Milk Dress

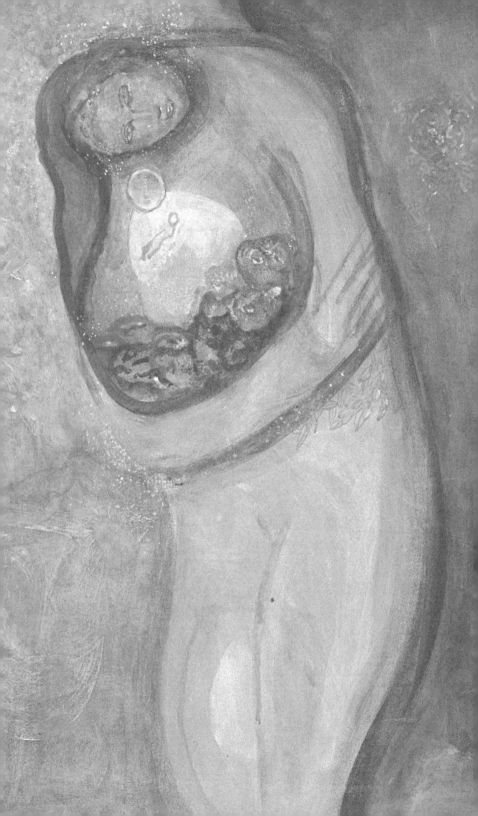

Milk Dress

POEMS BY

Nicole Cooley

ALICE JAMES BOOKS | FARMINGTON, MAINE

10 9 8 7 6 5 4 3 2 1

Alice James Books are published by Alice James Poetry Cooperative, Inc.,
an affiliate of the University of Maine at Farmington.

ALICE JAMES BOOKS
238 MAIN STREET
FARMINGTON, ME 04938

www.alicejamesbooks.org

Library of Congress Cataloging-in-Publication Data

Cooley, Nicole.
  Milk dress / Nicole Cooley.
    p. cm.
  ISBN 978-1-882295-83-8
  I. Title.

PS3553.O5647M55 2010
  811'.54--dc22

                              2010029322

Alice James Books gratefully acknowledges support from individual donors,
private foundations, the University of Maine at Farmington and the National
Endowment for the Arts. ❦

Cover art:
Louis Schneiderman, "Eve with Infant"
30 x 22"
Mixed media on paper
From the collection of Mary Ann Finn

Table of Contents

Acknowledgments

Some of these poems appeared in the following, sometimes under different titles and in slightly different versions:

The Journal of the Association for Research on Mothering: "Couplets Toward the Future," "Suitcase," "Objects in a Box for Class," "The cloth mother is heated," "The mother and fetus," "The eight newborn monkeys," "Always a murmur of Betadine and florescence," and "A sliver of dread"

Barrow Street: "Milk"

Not for Mothers Only: Contemporary Poems on Child-getting and Child-rearing, eds. Rebecca Wolff and Catherine Wagner: "Amniocentesis," "Cesarean," and "Pregnant at the Archive"

Womb: "Weaning," "Recto, Verso," and "Overlaying"

Under the Rock Umbrella: Contemporary Poets from 1951-1977, ed. William Walsh: "Self-portrait with Morning Sickness," "Hour of the Pink Flashlight," and "Triage Sonnet"

Poets on Place: Interviews and Tales from the Road, ed. W.T. Pfefferle: "Green Sandbox, Winter Sky"

Mississippi Review: "Damage Has Its Own Vocabulary," "Dr Spock's Common Sense Book of Baby and Child Care" (from "Three Documentaries"), and "Firstborn"

Washington Square: "Grief as Is"

Bellevue Literary Review: "Suspicion"

EPOCH: "Cesarean"

The Clarion: "Homeland Security"

Iris: A Journal About Women: "Ghazal of Nines"

Free Verse: A Journal of Contemporary Poetry and Poetics: "Triage Sonnet"

New England Review: "Pregnant at the Archive" and "Self-portrait with Morning Sickness"

Mem: "The Last Quatrains in the Ballad of the Bad Mother," "Firstborn," and "Amniocentesis"

"In the Anatomical Museum" was awarded the Emily Dickinson Award from the Poetry Society of America in 2006.

This would not be a book without Nancy Austin, Julia Bouwsma, Peter Cooley, Jacki Cooley, Joanna Fuhrman, Alissa Rowan, and Carey Salerno. And I am grateful to my colleagues at Queens College—The City University of New York and to all my students who remind me always to take risks.

Most of all, huge gratitude, for the inspiration of their life and work, to Julia Kasdorf and Kimiko Hahn.

And in memory of my grandmothers, Ruth Cooley and Anne Marks.

To my beloveds: Laban, Meridian, Arcadia.

A mother is a continuous separation, a division of the very flesh.
—Julia Kristeva, "Stabat Mater"

Marie's spilled her milk again. No use crying over spilled milk.
Wittgenstein says there is no such thing as a private language.
I think it would be worth trying to make one.
—Bernadette Mayer, *Midwinter Day*

Homeland Security

Write against narrative: here is the television's blue
square of light, milk needling my skin.

The September sky burns metal blue, each day's fabric
torn away from my window.

The television's stark horizontal. The city dimmed,
asphalt shaking with the subway's rush toward home.

Write toward the girl, asleep beside me, her body
made of mine.

The television's expanse of glass, its flat metallic voice,
its slur of headlines.

I hold the baby while jets cross and recross over this city.

The current threat advisory is—

Write against blankness, a sheet strung tight,
a bed the color of ash: white, white, white.

Self-portrait with Morning Sickness

Don't tell me the body's opposite is—

Winter rain stumbles at the window,
while in bed I rise and sink.

My body is its own shipwreck.
No map. No vision of the shore.

Just a slow undertow pulling me
away from my old life.

Across the room, my black dress takes
a hangar's shape, dividing past

from present, and I am nothing
but a ship of sickness,

split into pieces, scattered.
Inside my skin, another

body floats. Listen—the body's
opposite is not the spirit.

It is nothing but this wish.

The cloth mother is heated by a light bulb hidden

deep inside. She'll offer comfort but no nourishment. She'll offer her body wrapped with a towel. And the baby monkey will cling. The baby will turn from the other mother made of mesh, the other mother who is all hard edges who is offering her milk.

The macaque monkeys were removed from their mothers after birth for the experiment. For this purpose, we contrived two surrogate mother monkeys.

Inside the mother, the light bulb blinks and warms and casts its shadows.

Pregnant at the Archive

where you are not supposed to have a body
in Special Collections, in the straight-spined chair

where you study portraiture, Cassatt's late prints.
Directions: open each folder slowly, remove the proofs.

So many bathing scenes. All the private actions.
Inside your body, a ring of cells divides, divides.

Each image is a reprise. Fugitive red, fine
drypoint hatching to expose the mother's inked-in hair.

The child always underscored by absence of detail.
Directions: study the careful incision of lines.

Inside your body, the other is still safely separate.
Most often Cassatt leaves the background blank.

Directions: don't look down at yourself below the desk.
A pencil study. Drypoint outline. Aquatint.

Directions: will you remember the occupation
of just one self.

Cassatt reverses the terms of reproduction, copies
her finished oil.

Directions: will you remember.
Only the friction of two bodies that share an outline.

All the conflicting voices. The body backlit.
The body incidental. The body reprised.

Pencil study. Final print. Slow, familiar dissolution.

A Mother's face obscured.

Triage Sonnet

The self I tried to stamp out will come back,
but I don't know it yet. And I don't know
what's next, in this white room, the door just cracked
open enough to admit each long, low
moan from the next bed. Someone else's pain
floods the hall like light. Now, for once, I don't
write it down, don't step outside myself, brain
releasing body, my mind letting go
of everything but thought. Instead, I'm here,
at the edge of the corridor of dark,
praying out loud to no one, no one near:
after her birth, when I am split apart,
let she and I be one, bodies pressed together
like the pages of a book, unwritten, open forever.

Amniocentesis

the sky a lake in the New York barely
dark outside the bedroom window
the willow is all
            clusters bubbles foam disappearing

        like the body I've convinced
                    myself—chromosomes
                rearranging fiction
into fact   the hollow needle will reveal

            shuttered like a window   I wait

        let the world beneath the skin be pure
astonishment

O Body no matter what the sky leaks through

i.

The mother and fetus, Leonardo believed, exchanged their blood. When my daughter is sick, I feel heat rise in my own skin. I lie beside her, her fever leaking into me.

ii.

The first love of the human infant is for his mother. The tender intimacy of this attachment is such that it is sometimes regarded as a sacred or mystical force, an instinct incapable of analysis. No doubt such compunctions, along with the obvious obstacles in the way of objective study, have hampered experimental observation of the bonds between child and mother.

iii.

Which is a rope—

Which is a rope, snapping?

Which mother will lie awake all night, wishing for solitude, yet wishing for her daughters' small bodies wound into hers, while the radiator hisses, the dull gray color of a knife?

Cesarean

Now the irises rage light   spiked tongues
at the hospital window

How I would like to just unravel

Through glass   cut leaves curl like fingers
in my throat

I once wished to take myself apart

There is no space between us   body caught in my body

There is the voice telling me *there are many ways
to give birth*

The lesson chalked on the sidewalk,
these lines the surgeon sketches—

to save her   cut here and here and here

Three Documentaries

Photograph #1, The Lying-in Hospital

Past the Emergency Pavilion's bordered brick, over
a roundabout, through the revolving door's glass
triangles that refuse to scatter into shadow,
turn at the Diagnostic Imaging Center beside the sign,
etched in stone: *This Building Dedicated*
To the Well-Being of Mothers and Babies,
Anno Domini, 1928,
to the room where a sonogram machine spins
its own story, where language
skims the surface of the image and fails,
where at this moment someone
watches herself, singularity erased.

Photograph #2, Queensboro Bridge

The sky salt white. The rails scrawl
across the water, a barge piled high with tires.
First the shock that there's a world

beyond my body. First this landscape
outside the magnetic field I can't step into,
tube of light where my child lies,
small fists tied down, fairy-tale oven.
I don't want to see it, so I watch
the green black water, remember
a butterfly clip pinching a vein
open, needle of wicker-colored fluid
spilling my body's secrets, promising
faith. The only promise is that the self
will be crowded out of the body.
That the bridge scripts the river.

Photograph #3, Interior, Mother & Child

The road back to myself will be lined
with gravel, stuttered with dirt, running
through the family plots beyond the house,
Mother, Beloved Mother, all unnamed.
The other body within mine at first
not yet solid, not vapor. Then,
all afternoon the child surfaces from sleep
on the white bed, fastens herself to me.
One grave in the family plot repeated.

One body that is its own vanishing point.
This self that now fits only in the edges
of my life, this body that keeps making and
unmaking, taking in darkness, giving back light.

Suspicion

After Alfred Hitchcock

Return everything to image: a sonogram's Doppler
radar transforming echo into bone.

First vision of the girl a film still.

Blink, my eyes gritty with remembering. In the theater,
the baby breathes against my chest.

There is another world inside her skin.

Sleep is a flip-book opened and shut too fast.
Sleep is a door jammed shut.

Remembering the bed collapsing into a stretcher
at her birth, my body shuttered then thrown open.

The baby sleeps. I wait for the screen's rectangle
to reveal a dissolve.

Remembering I once read: the camera is a character,
the lens a voice.

Against me the girl stirs. I hold my breath.
On the screen the husband lies and lies,

the husband offers his wife the poison and what a
pleasure to believe him,

to let everything return to image:

a lit-up glass of milk glowing in the husband's hands,
a tiny bulb inside.

Firstborn

Who makes two into three. Who the dark unfastened and let go. Who joins me again to my own mother. In her glass bassinet, the baby is an exhibit of one, the baby is lit from within, the baby has no language, so I lift her up. I give her to my mother. Who am I speaking to? You, dragged from me into life. You, whose body opened to release mine. Who taught me the lesson: a woman becomes her mother. Who taught me how each body can reveal another. In the stories you read me, a daughter stays a daughter. Lost in a forest, floor of dirt dark velvet, inside a tower, encircled by rock walls. A daughter is forever an empty corridor. Who taught the magic: center stage, while the magician waits, the woman flattens her body on a white bed. Trick accomplished. The surgeon cuts the body in two, and a girl steps out, curtsies to the crowd. The secret is the moment when the daughter holds her own daughter, when the mother stands beside the bed. The secret of this trick is mirrors: mother reflecting daughter reflecting daughter reflecting—

In the Blue Exam Book After the Birth Because I Was Told to Write Everything Down

For Kimiko

i.

Pink bulb of Tylenol to stick in the baby's mouth.
Cold spoon to hold on her gums to soothe her.
Let her suck on your finger all night.

ii.

You might want to know if I miss the friction
of bodies, your shirt, cotton skimming my ribs.
The tea was passionfruit, pooling in a saucer.
The tea stewed cherry, so thick
I couldn't drink it.
Yes, I am afraid to bathe her.

iii.

Cell by cell the baby made herself, the cells
Made cells. Made largely of milk.

iv.

Feeding 2, 4, 10. Diaper 3, 5.
Check for fever, check for wetness,
check for breathing with
a square of Kleenex above her mouth.

v.

transfusion

vi.

A pot of tea, blood red, served to my friend
visiting the baby.

The baby trying to get back inside my body.
Diamond tiles in the apartment bathroom
the color of milk,
my face against the cold sink, and the baby cries
in a bouncy seat outside the door.

On the kitchen table a browning apple
cut open for no one.

Grief as Is

In memory of Ruth Cooley

A silver gift bag holds the box of ashes beside my bed.
In the closet, flushed, buttery silk. Clothes tell her story,
how fifty years ago the Empire Builder sped to this city
where I yank her jacket, fingernail pink, tight across
my breasts, I pretend I'm her, while Fifth Avenue
floods with light. Where I pretend I'm her

—Italian Pavilion New York 100% Merino Wool—

and pretend she isn't dead, stand at the closet door, step
into her dress, black acetate shimmering stiff.
Clothes hold me together. Labels a narrative of events

—Miss Liberty Fashions Madison Avenue
60% Gabardine 40% Nylon—

I try everything on. Grief's landscape is fabric:
small cigarette burn on a sleeve or
an edge of stained eyelet lace. Mourning is repair:
holding the silver needle, thread wet with spit
as I stitch all the holes shut.

i.

The eight newborn monkeys have their own cages, with equal access to a cloth and a wire mother.

ii.

If I wanted to stay with her, I was told to put on the lead dress.

My daughter wore a blue-sprigged hospital gown. I was not allowed to hold her. I tried to soothe her but the lead collar choked my voice out of my throat.

Stabat Mater, Fragments

i.

The water is iconic.
Imagine this scene sketched out in charcoal,

in pencil, in sidewalk chalk.
In the tub, the girl reaches for the faucet's silver fistful.

The girl I once harbored
in my body. Now she is all expectancy. I lift her in.

ii.

*Once upon a time, I will not tell her, I practiced being pure
object, I divided myself from myself, I arranged my body at
the river's edge. Picture the levee in summer light. Picture a
man waiting behind the trees, a camera in his hands.*

iii.

Once the girl was image, a sonogram's slur of dark and
light, mapped in the water of my body.

iv.

The water is a bedsheet   The water's surface is
onionskin   asphalt   burlap

v.

Once upon a time, I was proud of my own emptiness. I
emptied myself of all desire. Someone touched me but no
one could touch me. This was, of course, before the girl
broke my circumference.

vi.

Once upon a time this girl was image. Now she is pure
motion: morning light flares through her skin,
her hands breaking, unbreaking
a bubbled surface with delight.

vii.

The water is a screen door slamming in another city when I
run out of the house. Sun loosens the dirt at the Mississippi's
edge and the stones the river gives back are cool beads of light.
I sit without moving on the bank. Stillness keeps you safe.

Here is a lesson I won't hand down to my daughter.

viii.

This girl loves water, loves its arms around her,
its crystalline.
Imagine her posed on makeshift velvet.
Imagine her at another river's edge.

ix.

Arms crossed over my chest, I knew I was already dead, they
had dredged me up from the river bottom, the nurse swathed
dirt from my hair, someone rolled my body on a rubber sheet,
under the eye of the surgical lamp.

x.

Not the amniotic.
Not the water that divides self from self.

And the camera's lens blinks open between the trees.

xi.

the water veiling   the water assessing its own level
the water reversing time

xii.

I lift her out. I breathe her in. I press my mouth
to her hair. She loosens against my chest,
reaches her arms around my neck.

The water resists the story,
and years from now I will not know her body.

Couplets Toward the Future

Now each day is a gasp. A helicopter stutters
across the blank blue sky, then disappears

into the city's empty horizon, air clear
of smoke that sometimes rises, sometimes disappears,

jaundiced smell filling our bedroom with fear
of the future. That day won't disappear—

it's always replayed as "America's New War,"
this century's lesson: how bodies disappear—

war started in the city where our family began, here,
where the best is waking, all dark disappeared,

where the baby lies between us we breathe her
in, and I want the world outside to disappear.

It won't. It shouldn't. And as we hold each other,
pull our daughter closer, I think of The Disappeared.

I used to ask how my body made another. Last year's
question. Now, I ask you, how can a body disappear?

Your hands hold me. In the unmapped future,
I will refuse to let the three of us disappear.

Overlaying

All that first September with my daughter, I wanted the world to turn safely miniature: the baby finally asleep, the book open on my lap.

Outside the train shuddered along the horizon, the National Guard patrolled, guns slung on their shoulders, grass scattered with trash beside the Halal Market.

Everyone said: don't sleep with the baby. Too dangerous. Keep your distance.

As if the book could cancel the world, I read:

in another century a mother's body broke open again and again. Her seventh child, another boy, she sets to

sleep beside her, body slick with his sweat, with hers. All
night she watched him, eyes gritty with exhaustion, while
outside in the fields the war went on, war that took her
husband, that could take her son.

On the subway on the way home from my night
class, my chest burning, breasts heavy with milk, on
the subway on the way home to feed the baby, on the
subway, stopped again, the police walking through each
car, on the subway stopped again for Police Action or
Random Backpack Searching.

The infant rocked in his mother's arms as if she were a
wooden chest. As if she were a boat.

A boat filling with water.

Then the baby shifted on my lap. I set her down to sleep
beside me, breathed in her salt-smell. Uncurled her fists,
flattened her fingers, tendrils and roots, over the sheets.

That fall, I wasn't writing, but a book always had its own rhythms in my hands: the book the page the paragraph the sentence the word the word the word equaling or at least promising safety,

If I stepped outside that circle of light, there was always the television, the new war repeating. No safe distance.

In the book, the mother imagined a child requiring nothing. What if he choked on his own breath? What if she dragged the quilt over his body? What if a small body shuddered shut? She closed her eyes. Her eyes were burning.

Outside, another helicopter circled the sky. I lay down next to the baby.

The word made flesh. For nothing?

The woman could just lie down beside, along, on top of, the child. She could cover the child with her body. Drown out his cries with the press of her mouth. She could lie and lie and lie and in the morning it would be over —

☙

That fall, I told my class: change your writing by changing the space of your writing

and I gave them tiny notebooks, paper grocery bags, sheets of newsprint telling stories of the war, and I explained the origins of the palimpsest, lines overlaying lines,

and I said, erase your own words with your words, and the baby breathed and

breathed and outside the other world wouldn't stop tunneling through this one.

Always a murmur of Betadine and florescence. My arms
not mine but blue-sheeted
in the operating theater where each moment telescopes—

I want someone to offer comfort.
Recovery room: baby wrapped in a receiving blanket
the color of a bruise.

Pedagogy, 2001

The burning drifts in our apartment window, hangs
in the air, a long, low hum.

Call it the white space, the page's visual field, I used to tell
my class. *Write the poem you have been avoiding all semester.*

The missing described by their tattoos, birthmarks,
scars. The poems taped to the fence in Union Square.

"E Train to World Trade," the intercom announces.
I take my place on the train through Queens.

After the planes hit, at first, the university insisted, *you
will be teaching. Classes will be held as scheduled today.*

The missing described: The father who worked
for the Port Authority as a fire-fighter.
The cousins, undocumented workers, who did not
come home that day.

*We can't discuss the Rukeyser poem because it is too
painful*, I tell my class. But talking about the poem
is what they want to do.

We are told to make a stockpile in our small
apartment: gas masks, antibiotics, cash, food and water
to last several weeks.

It's not that language has limits, as I was taught, but
that it is bottomless.

Half the poetry workshop went downtown to give
blood, to volunteer as translators.

Mass transit on high alert. All tunnels closed.

✚

In office hours, my student tells me the missing woman
from Windows on the World has her name,
shows me the flyer.

✚

Flags are hung everywhere in this neighborhood,
on the car service dashboard,
on the door of the Halal Market.

✚

We're Generation 9/11, my student says.

✚

Write the poem, I insist. A few miles away are the fires,
still burning.

✚

How can I tell them: *walk to the edge of the blank space
of the page.*

The dye would be injected. Her body would be illuminated till it is sparkled, glittered, till the large machine was lowered much too close to her skin. She and I would have to stay in the hospital room until the doctors could strap her down, her body pinned to the table like an insect, spread-eagled, her small body ready and opened.

Removed from their mothers at their births. Deprived of touch. And none will want the mother offering milk.

The Last Quatrains
in the Ballad of the Bad Mother

After Gwendolyn Brooks

The bad mother plays movie star suicide while
her baby sleeps on the christening pillow,
then dreams her escape, laddering out
the nursery window, down alone to the neon street.

She kisses the baby on the lips, on the shuttered blue
eyes, on the pouch of a mouth, body once the size
of a fist. She can't stop rehearsing
loss. Body that now in our world she can't keep safe.

Damage Has Its Own Vocabulary

The ones who died of childbed fever   foreheads
sponged and glistening   bodies caught in other bodies
the ones uncomforted   floor scored with voices   births
cut short and shrinking light   quarantine door shut
coupled windows closed   ice clotting in the grass as
winter unspools   no one can tell me how to speak in
another language   my love for her a skillet riven with oil
unshoveled front walk where any of us could fall

Weaning

Another night like the glassine surface
    of a lake and she and I gone
        under.
                In the kitchen I unlatch
    the plastic clasp of my nursing bra,
    prepare to watch

    the second year of the war on television.
In its blue light,
    objects glow on the table—a ring of toast,
a medicine bulb, the distance
    I've traveled from myself.
           Sharp focus on another life,

on what our country has done:
        "Shock and Awe." Here is the baby
        the same age as the war.

Out the window she watches silver coins of rain
    and I hold her
    closer as we slip under the surface
        of the world, under the meniscus

of a glass of water held in shaking hands.

We can't stay there. Change the channel:

a child lies in the street, cinder and ash
              while the president warns
                                of "grave danger."
while I remember the pregnancy test
I took the first night
        of the bombing, TV landscape

                flashing yellow, lit by lasers
so America at home could watch a city be destroyed:

"There will not be a safe place in Baghdad when we attack."
        Now
two years later we know there was no threat.
        We do not count dead civilians.
                        Now my daughter's body
will begin
              loosening from mine.
We will rise up into what is unseeable. We have no choice.

Suitcase

Gold-zippered, blue plaid, gilded with initials: suitcase
we were told to *pack in case of a new attack*. Girl's suitcase,

my grandmother's gift for those first sleepovers.
I fill it with duct tape. *Cipro* hidden in the the suitcase.

The pediatrician refused but, yes, I begged, cried.
In the *Before*, this would be my daughter's suitcase.

While she slept inside me, I'd pack each silky nightie.
In the third trimester, I'd lie in bed and arrange the suitcase.

Now: Swiss Army knife. Distilled water. Potassium iodide
to carry with us at all times, in case of—

tablets to swallow as the subway fills with smoke.
This city permanently on *Orange Alert*, the ready suitcase

waiting while I nurse my daughter, watch the news.
In the *After*, another day of jewel blue sky, I pack the suitcase,

seal the windows, as told, against *possible chemical attack*,
but still we breathe in the burning, the ash, the soot.

Plan an evacuation route. The city shuts tunnels,
cuts us off. We're packed and ready, with our suitcase.

I watch the news. I already know I won't have another child.
Packed and ready for the next attack: our suitcase.

You must be ready, the TV tells us. *To leave your life,
for the safety of your family.* I lay my daughter in the suitcase

stamped with my initials, N.R.C., letters engraved long ago
on a headstone, and now not mine, not hers, no one's suitcase.

Disaster, an Instruction Manual

Keep them from the news. Turn off the television.

Never let them see the computer screen in your study with its images of smoke or water or ash.

Always whisper when you talk to your husband in the kitchen or your sister on the phone.

After school, while I slice apple, pour sippy cups of milk, Meridian sits at the table, construction paper fanned across its surface. She scratches her crayon hard on the paper. *There's a hurricane in Arcadia's town, and I'm trying to save her.*

Disaster: *from the Italian, disastro, meaning "ill-starred," from dis—"away, without," and astro, "star, planet" from the Latin.*

My father stands in the late fall dark of our backyard in New Jersey with a pack of matches. *Look,* he says, and lights up the MRE, military-issued food he and my mother were given by the National Guard.

My daughters are watching from the back steps. I want to imagine the scene is somehow lovely, a shower of sparkles in the backyard grass.

Five minutes after leaving the apartment, my husband calls home from a pay phone. *Someone just told me there's been a plane crash at the World Trade Center. Turn on the TV.*

In the rocking chair, my daughter on my lap, breast-feeding her before I leave, my first reaction is grip her so tightly she wakes up and begins to cry.

Disaster: *mischance, misfortune, misadventure, mishap*
Disaster: *a total failure*

You want to go down to New Orleans but you can't. It's not just that they won't let anyone in the city—no rentry is allowed—but you can't leave your children.

You want to save your parents but you can't. All you can do is watch the news, the city filling like a bowl.

⚜

Disaster: *a calamitous event; a sudden loss of life; a business failure*

⚜

How to make it beautiful? How to keep them safe?

⚜

We can't have another child, I tell my husband.

⚜

On the N-train, potassium iodide tablets safely stashed in my book bag, next to the books of poetry I plan to teach in class, I sit in my plastic seat trying not to look at anyone around me. *If you see something, say something*, the posters entreat. As if it is important to be suspicious of everyone around you, at all times, but at the same time not to look too closely at them.

⚜

Disaster, now obsolete: *an unfavorable aspect of a star or planet.*

The morning of the hurricane, I placed my last phone call with my parents. We all knew Katrina would be a direct hit, and it would likely be a Category Five storm. *You have got to leave,* I told them. *Go to the Superdome.* They would not listen.

The truth is, I know now, it was already far too late for them to leave the city.

How to turn it into a lesson?

Disaster, an alphabet: *act of God, adversity, affliction, bad luck, bad news, bale, bane, blight, blow, bust, calamity, casualty, cataclysm, catastrophe, collapse, collision, crash, debacle, defeat, depression, emergency, exigency, failure, fall, fell stroke, fiasco, flood, flop, grief, hard luck, harm, hazard, holocaust, hot water, ill luck, misadventure, mischance, misfortune, mishap, reverse, rock, rough, ruin, ruination, setback, slip, stroke, the worst, tragedy, undoing, upset, washout, woe.*

Green Sandbox, Winter Sky

In the middle of the yard, my daughter fills her dress
with sand as if she can ground herself in the earth

I watch her from the cracked back step while the baby
waits in me undone   unfinished   unready

I want to believe in language fastening each moment to
the present

Her turtle sandbox I anchored with stones
her gingham dress

She sifts dead grass through her fingers under the sky
white as paper where nothing is written

The driveway's black macadam   lawn filmed with milk

Here is a scene in which I can't plot myself
as the heroine

while the iris bulbs I planted for her knit and twist
under the dirt

The one unborn and the one who already belongs
to the world   not to me

Objects in a Box for Class

i.

Baby teeth I wrapped in plastic. Jar of Play-Doh.
A tiny ball, its rubber skin slit.
Describe, I tell the students. *Inhabit. I want you to become
your object.*

ii.

At the block party, alone at the edge of the fence,
I watch the girls scratch at clotted winter grass
with a fork, a piece of glass.

Alone: the card table in the yard laid
with the children's gifts: lensless glasses,
Kleenex flower, this junk they've dug up from the dirt.

Alone. The other mothers inside with beer.

Other mothers don't watch, don't want to make
the moment what it's not—

iii.

I hate you, my daughter whispers
from her blue car seat.

iv.

Their crying: beads on a necklace split, spilling, coming
undone.

Their crying: beads rolling away from me,
under the rug.

The beads scatter in the box. Glass marbles or sleeping
pills I won't take.

v.

Five days home with my daughters, five days of fevers,
cold baths, wrung-out washcloths on foreheads, pink-
bulbed Tylenol to squirt inside cheeks, I only want to
smoke. Then to smash the cigarette on the asphalt.

vi.

If you don't like your object, I tell my class. *You still have to write.* You don't get to choose.

vii.

The other mothers don't sit in a web of dirt in the yard with their children, watching.

viii.

Alone: *don't leave me, don't let her, don't make me.* My four year old snaps a rubber band over and over against her wrist in the bed beside me while her sister twists in a fever sleep. *Don't touch me.* I press the cold washcloth on my older daughter's face. I unfold it, wring it, pack it with ice again.

Don't leave.

ix.

"The Inaccessible Object of Desire," name of a French class I took in college.

Object of the gaze. (Eyes like the bottom of a blue glass bottle.)

Transitional object: breast, bottle, pacifier, my ring finger they sucked and chewed.

Objects I collected from their playroom and brought on the subway to school.

x.

The objects sleep in their box. The girls dig in the dirt.

It's unmothering Sunday and I stretch out alone in my bed, naked under an old crib sheet.

Where are the daughters? I prepare myself by pretending they're already gone. They've already left me. I practice the separation of mother and infant.

And none will want the mother, offering milk.

Breastfeeding at the Harvard Club

under a photo of T.S. Eliot and Vivian knocking
cocktails together, the baby on my lap.

In the Commonwealth Room, under the gaze of the waiters,
the baby twists under the *Boston Globe* I've tented over us.

Try to think abstractions. Outside, a fountain
choked with blinding silver white, the shiniest dimes.

Brunch drifts on without me, the baby twisting
my nipple until it burns. A tower of salmon and crushed

ice, champagne flutes. Try to think. My mind is a shuttered
window, snapped and sealed against light. I'll never return

to the table. While she feeds, the baby rests her fingers
on my tongue. I'm tired of the poet's own voice

but can't recall any others. Just an instrument,
this body I haven't practiced. Eliot smiles,

sips his drink and I'd like to knock the circle of daisies
to the floor. I'd like to write about the Women's Entrance

Vivian used. I'd like to write about silence, to flip
on searchlights to sweep the drawing room,

and set every corner burning. And here is my daughter's
hand inside my mouth. No metaphor can transport

me into the water of that fountain.
Or inside the glittering display of ice.

Three Documentaries

Dr Spock's Common Sense Book of Baby and Child Care

The afternoon is an unmade bed you can't crawl into.

Fever flares through the baby's skin, cries fluent with anger, but you can't touch her. You can't leave the rocker where you sit alone. Her cries won't stop. You turn from her, watch the night-light glow cold as a diamond, and take yourself somewhere else: the bed, a covered wagon lists out to the prairie. The bed floats on glass wheels into the sky.

You no longer rise up to panic, breasts prickling with milk. Instead you rock without her until you are a strip of sidewalk, a loose board under this room.

Her cry is an edge of wire stretching through your body but you don't feel it.

Her cries are a staircase you won't climb.

Phillip Wylie's Generation of Vipers

Catastrophe: the sacrament shocks
you with a new vocabulary. It's mid-
century, and *Mom is a human calamity.*
Dream girl, pin-up, metal breasts
swaying as she enters your room
to warn you. *Chrome-plated agate eyes
embedded in cement.* Caution:
Mom is dangerous. Watch her
as she crouches along your sidewalk
skyline, ten years after the war.
Watch her: *Medusa, Pandora, Queen
of Hell.* Remember: once your body caught
in hers. She would not let go.

Jean Piaget's The Language and Thought of the Child

In the beginning was the word and the word was the
mother's body

In the beginning were our whispers   syllables like cut-out
girls hands linked

In the beginning was all prosody   pure intonation
strung beads of light

In the beginning no *I* but nevertheless a lexicon
More + X   Want + X

In the beginning were our questions   Is milk a word   Is
silence

In the beginning phrases nest like Russian dolls mother
inside daughter

And now   after her voice is alive in the world outside my
body   a chain letter

a sentence   sent and sent and sent

Milk

I am being broken open—

a woman sits in a garden, holds hank
of red to edge, skein of blue,

tongue sealing each small knot of each
doll dress and through the window,

behind glass, her children: wanting.
Now, at the estate sale, all those clothes

drift in a laundry basket, price-tagged.
I bend down to touch them, but

my girl says, *Carry me*, lifts her arms
to reach. I imagine that woman casting off,

starting a shell-stitch and I fill
a grocery bag—doll nightgowns, booties,

tiny hats, ribbon-threaded. I have to set
my daughter down to cry. That other

mother is a perfect still life. Soap carving.
Plastic Virgin Mary night-light I once

bought as a joke. She loops and winds
her yarn and never feels that deep

blue bottomless lake of a child's too
much wanting. Her lesson is:

How to Keep and Discard.
Save a tiny butter colored sweater.

Sailor dress piped in pink with mother
of pearl buttons. Save this girl who once

lived safely in my body, now spilling
from my lap, fingers in my hair,

girl crying for me while I hold her.
Forget this dark, clotted center of myself,

crushed red plum of anger. Save that woman
in the garden, folding and unfolding

clothes alone while light lies
broken on porch stones. Save the clothes

spread around us on the floor. Save this girl
I love so fiercely but still leave her.

Forget my anger boiling over like milk
on a stove. Save a blue

and white ceramic pitcher on a table,
empty, clean, poured out.

Hour of the Pink Flashlight

Ice clinks in glasses that answer each other
but at the bottom
of mine is a mouthful of sand. I've gone down—
Hour of the Bucket and Shovel.
Hour of the Bubble Wand.
What did you bring from the other world?

These two small girls asleep in our bed upstairs.
Hour of the Blind Swing Set.
Hour of Sidewalk Chalk Anointing.
Last night rain blistered the asphalt and we lay
together as I repeated that line from a song: I am hard to love.

I repeated: I am better at being disembodied.
Hour of the Wading Pool.
Hour of the Slide's Metal Tongue.
What is the lesson?
How to be a stranger to yourself. How all it takes

is the smallest shift in your visual field: the two girls sleeping
beside each other, two girls who once lived in my body.
On the lawn, my dress is pillowcase white.

Hour of Collision. Hour of Proximity and Surplus.
Hour of Overlap.

What do I want, secretly?
How to be a woman in a cocktail dress walking expertly past
our house. How to love an act and its embodiment.

How to love the pair of orange lilies that bang their bodies
against the fence.

Which is a rope—

Which is a rope, snapping?

*Which mother will lie awake all night while the moon
hangs low, too close?*

Dress on a Wire Hanger
with Ink, Wax, Thread

After "Poem Hair Dress" by Lesley Dill

Fabric flares in the backyard grass where I stitch, snip,
stencil edges of a dress.
Inside me now, a girl unspools, my Infanta,
miniature princess spinning on a doll stand.
I want a dress to convince me:
there is always a body in another body.
I want a dress that will not run
through my fingers like clear water.
A dress to mark how often I used to startle out
of myself.
Word made flesh. A dress that is all friction.

First, one child. Girl in a christening dress.
One girl stitches, stencils. Knits, snips, stains, drizzles
cold tea on satin.
One girl's signature on my skin. But twice
my body will grind shut then open.
I finger the skirt, all tulle, all white, all
ruffled, stuffed.

Once the dress floats, it's shaken loose,
comes to rest below the fence
where my babies sleep in the grass.
The two girls and I will lie
together, dress dividing space
between us, separating past and present.
Dress that is not a backdrop.
Dress that makes the other world visible.
Lesson Dress. *Dress of Flesh.*
Dress refusing Empty.

Recto, Verso

A seam in the dirt divides past from present:
rope I once set down

             in the sand of the levee, or the girls
        asleep in our bed

        with me between them,

girls who want stories that forecast their presence.

I should tell how I brought them here,

                after the storm,
how we stood between the levee and the house,

on River Road,
            how we walked along the floodwall,
        tangled branches, dirt

yellow-rusted while the river was still silvering,
a clench
of sunlight. I wouldn't let them touch
            the trees, the rocks, the sticks.

Make this scene a book open on a table:
the dirt, the water. A page

ripped out. A mud bank, this river's splintered
light, its crystal. I left that city.

I stood up, I walked away—

                    And the city cracked open. And
          the city flooded.

In bed, now, here
are two pages joined together. I hold my girls,

          girls who won't remember
this, how I am pressed between them
like a leaf on tracing paper.

Ghazal of Nines

If skin is a map as we lie side by side, today marks nine
times I've traced our journey since that day: ninth

afternoon of another January, your hand caught
in mine as we pledged each other to each other, nine

now our number for luck. All that long year after—
as if the ocean that separated us could spin nine

times into rope to hold us, as if the earth's underground
rooms could tunnel us together for nine

more hours, minutes, seconds. We didn't know
we'd live here in this city. We didn't know nine

months would spin into another life, this girl who
brims with delight when we kiss each other. Now nine

years are threads of the future, knotted, braided, loomed
together, marriage a fabric that covers us as nine

marks the day we swore to save each other. Now knock
on the bedpost nine times for luck. Oh Kingdom of Nines,

be our map, our signature, as our bodies hold each other
tight on this bed, this canvas, this paper, this ninth—

Milk Dress

For Julia

Corsets kept a woman breathless—

The crying spills over a shoulder, over the edge of a spoon.
The crying is shaking silver.

Now the daughters downstairs. And I sit
in my room reading. No transport—a book static, open, flat.

The crying will be given back to me because I've left,
because I sit at the window without them in a white dress.

☥

Body turned inside out, not the black maternity suit my
friend and I shared two separate winters as each body
reached the moment when there was only doubling,
when there was just this black suit so much more precise
than language, that could conceal, reveal, black suit we
mailed back and forth between us, daughters we hold till
there is no space between us, black suit that shaped its
own landscape.

⚜

Hospital gown open up the back, coverlet of stars—

⚜

One in the stroller, one in my arms

⚜

Less a *breath* than a shudder, the baby latches on
and in the dressing room we sink together

below the surface of the afternoon, a heap of
silk and acetate and wool I won't try on.

Milk under my skin like a gas stove's hidden blue
hum, under a too-tight lace and wire bra.

⚜

Pregnant—as if I shucked a dress off my shoulders
and stepped into this other, this another

⚜

Or, out on the city street, I say now, forget
the dress, we walk towards home and I

hold both girls in my arms, none left

in my body, my skin still tight and hot.
I'm all sharp-edged blossoms bordering

a hem, a sleeve, I'm a field of white, or
we walk and walk and I clasp them close to me,

so tight none of us can breathe.

In the Anatomical Museum

The Mütter Museum, Philadelphia

Past a skull collection, model of a gangrene hand
to the "Plates Illustrative of a Treatise on Midwifery, 1813"—

Leonet forceps, decapitating hook "used to extract
the child by the head from the maternal passage."

Or the umbilical cord with 26 twists. Or the placenta
molded from paraffin. I am looking for the Labor Scene.

Not the instruments: blade, shank, lock: but
women holding each other, women delivering—

Not my dream last night that I was pregnant
for the third time but there was no baby,

no "obstetrical interventions" to remove this body
from my body. I would not go down to that place

I'd traveled twice. I would not return to Cervidil,
Pitocin drip, to the birthing room where I had failed,

lifted off the bed on a rubber sheet and wheeled
to the surgical theater where nurses tied down my hands

76

where I breathed the plastic shell of an oxygen mask.
On the second floor the curator draped

a wax model in muslin to resemble a patient on a table,
body for the surgeon to unfold. That place I'd traveled—

a hundred years ago I would not have come back—
Now my two girls running on the lawn beyond

the museum, behind the black gate, my girls
who cannot be bodiless.

A sliver of dread. A slash and then the baby is small enough to fit underneath the surface of my skin where I can keep her safe forever.

The dye they injected was pale purple. The dye was green and I was not allowed to hold her.

The baby was lost then found under a cabbage leaf, silky as a gown on a wedding night, white as spilled milk.

Portions of the text in the italicized untitled sections throughout the book are borrowed from Harry F. Harlow, "Love in Infant Monkeys," *Scientific American* 200 (June 1959).

Text in section iii. of "In the Blue Exam Book After the Birth Because I Was Told to Write Everything Down" uses language from George Oppen's poem "Sara in Her Father's Arms."

RECENT TITLES FROM ALICE JAMES BOOKS

Parable of Hide and Seek, Chad Sweeney
Shahid Reads His Own Palm, Reginald Dwayne Betts
How to Catch a Falling Knife, Daniel Johnson
Phantom Noise, Brian Turner
Father Dirt, Mihaela Moscaliuc
Pageant, Joanna Fuhrman
The Bitter Withy, Donald Revell
Winter Tenor, Kevin Goodan
Slamming Open the Door, Kathleen Sheeder Bonanno
Rough Cradle, Betsy Sholl
Shelter, Carey Salerno
The Next Country, Idra Novey
Begin Anywhere, Frank Giampietro
The Usable Field, Jane Mead
King Baby, Lia Purpura
The Temple Gate Called Beautiful, David Kirby
Door to a Noisy Room, Peter Waldor
Beloved Idea, Ann Killough
The World in Place of Itself, Bill Rasmovicz
Equivocal, Julie Carr
A Thief of Strings, Donald Revell
Take What You Want, Henrietta Goodman
The Glass Age, Cole Swensen
The Case Against Happiness, Jean-Paul Pecqueur
Ruin, Cynthia Cruz
Forth A Raven, Christina Davis
The Pitch, Tom Thompson
Landscapes I & II, Lesle Lewis
Here, Bullet, Brian Turner
The Far Mosque, Kazim Ali
Gloryland, Anne Marie Macari
Polar, Dobby Gibson
Pennyweight Windows: New & Selected Poems, Donald Revell
Matadora, Sarah Gambito
In the Ghost-House Acquainted, Kevin Goodan
The Devotion Field, Claudia Keelan

Alice James Books has been publishing poetry since 1973 and remains one of the few presses in the country that is run collectively. The cooperative selects manuscripts for publication primarily through regional and national annual competitions. Authors who win a Kinereth Gensler Award become active members of the cooperative board and participate in the editorial decisions of the press. The press, which historically has placed an emphasis on publishing women poets, was named for Alice James, sister of William and Henry, whose fine journal and gift for writing went unrecognized during her lifetime.

Typeset and Designed by
Pamela A. Consolazio

Printed by Thomson-Shore
on 30% postconsumer recycled paper
processed chlorine-free